Pen Painting Worlds

Anika Hossain

Presentation by *BookLeaf Publishing*

Web: www.bookleafpub.com

E-mail: info@bookleafpub.com

ISBN: 9789357744898

First edition 2023

ACKNOWLEDGEMENT

Thank you readers for giving this collection a chance. Thank you to folks who have no idea about this. Surprise! Lastly, thank you to my friends who gave me endless support. You are amazing and give me inspiration. I'm lucky to have had an opportunity to know you. I should have consulted with you guys as I was having a creative block writing this collection but regardless, thank you.

Playtime

I carry it around with me
 That drawing you made
 With all of the vibrant colours
 You colorued my dark shirt with the brightest
pink
 Gave me the strangest hair
 Made me more colourful than I truly was

We played make pretend
We could be whoever we wanted
You had the biggest laugh
Filling up the whole room
Your laughter is like a lullaby
Playing loudly over the noise within me
Drowning out my sorrow

You said aloud,
"More fun"
With your hand wrapped around my finger
My eyes started to well up
Such simple words
Carried with a big voice
Stirred such emotions

I'll try

Make time so we can play
I don't want to make empty promises
But I'll do my best to carry on
The train is just a few stops away
You won't have to wait for so long
I'm coming home to you
Our imagination will run free
And we shall play

Lucky Cap

It's late around the afternoon
I have to pick up a couple more shifts
Someday I won't have to work like this
I won't be so restless
Tired on the train
I won't have to work this late

I have to remind myself
It's not just me
It's for them
I'll work hard
They would want me to live on

To get a new pair of shoes
But the torn soles,
Where from the time of running around
Climbing trees
As you went higher by each branch

Describing the skyline
From the clouds,
 to the colour of the buildings
Trying to not fall from the great height
As I try not to fall into a slumber

Don't worry I'll be okay
I'll be coming home late
But I'm thinking of you
I've got your lucky hat
I wear it all day
So don't worry about me

Window Seat

I'll take the window seat
Inside the train
Watching the trees pass by me
Moving by so fast
Just like the thoughts in my head

I'm tired
My thoughts are always racing
Like the wheels on the track
So much noise
I just want a moment of silence

I don't know how long I can go on
But I'll have to go on to the next day
Hope my shoes don't break down
They're my favorite pair
Given to me by one who used to be here

She was kind
Taught me to embrace my emotions
To feel my anger
To feel my sadness
Not be bottled up inside

I wish I knew how to move on

To embrace change
Do I have to say goodbye?
Will she answer?
My eyelids start to fall
I'll dream of her in my sleep

Three Peas in a Pod

If you look around
 There's always something there
 Bits and pieces making up a scene
 Parts of a puzzle,
 being put together
 A story untold
 Ready to be shared

What's stopping you?
Don't be afraid to share
For a story to be told,
You must first let the idea free
Let it run wild
Your mind is not the only place for it to be

Are you afraid of not having an audience?
I wouldn't worry about that
You'll always have a supporter
One that's always there
One who is with you through thick and thin
That person is you

Worry not if your ideas are not good
Everyone must have a start somewhere
Try, fail, try again

Don't stop at 3 attempts
Keep going
Give it more that 3 chances
It doesn't have to be good if it's just for you

Find inspiration anywhere
From a bird on the street
To 3 passengers on a train
Sat next to each other
Like three peas in a pod

Take those coincidences
Make them into the story
Don't be afraid to create

Pockets of Peace

Some days are just rough
No matter how hard you try to be okay
Obstacles of thrown in your way
They're meant to hurt you
Meant to ruin your day

Trying to pass it
But there's potholes in the road
Leading you away from your destination
You try to focus
But your mind is in disarray

All you want is some peace
For all the negativity to just leave
It's been a long, long day
You're doing your best
It's okay to not be okay

You keep reminding yourself that
But words alone doesn't make you feel any
better
You rummage around
To see what you can find
In your pockets you find a bit of peace

Pockets of peace
A little time out of your day
To do something you enjoy
To make you feel okay

Elementals

You choose not to believe in yourself
You think you are unworthy of any title
You are nothing
You are worthless
That is what you believe

But I see you differently
You a person who tries
A person who may be afraid
But will still remain to shine bright
Your fears don't dim your light

So many things make up you
All with a beginning and an end
The ideas rough, unrefined
Like tools made of sticks
Then stone

Through a process
They are worked on
Eventually to be made of metal and fire
Created to be used
To serve
To help

Made up elementals
Varying in differences
But used to create
So can you

Between the Lines

"That's a good book"
A voice above my shoulder says
Their eyes glimmer with excitement,
Reaching the book to give to me
Carrying out the duty of the blurb on the back
Telling me the details with such delight

Reciting a line,
My interest is peaked
I wonder how simple lines on a page,
Gives them as much joy as it does
To have a twinkle in their eyes
As the sounds fall out their mouth
Traveling its way through my ears
To my mind

A place like this is special
It can be found anywhere
Holding so many stories, memories
It doesn't cost a dime
Take a look inside
Give a bit of your time

You'll meet many characters
All unique

As well as similar
Take your pick
Travel away
You'll hardly notice the hours passing by

You'll see yourself here
Your heart will ache
As you see their pain
Your heart will rejoice
As they finally do what you've been rooting for

Pick up a story
You won't be the first to read it
Nor will you be the last
You leave a piece of you between the pages
As you take a piece with you
Filling the pages to be thicker than they once
were
These stories are carried with you
As you write your own story

Creative Block

Blank
It's blank
My eyes are met with a page of nothing-ness
A blank page
A blank canvas
Empty notes
Nothing comes to mind

It's a normal thing
To be stuck
It's hard to create
When nothing comes to mind
I'm grasping for ideas like air

Creativity, like a source of freshwater
Limited but oh so valuable
Pumping the lever just to get a sip
What do I do when the tap barely drips?
Nothing comes out

I'm ready to drown
Ready to be engulfed in freshwater
To have creativity back in my system
But the water is shallow
I won't lay faced down

In attempt to be struck with creativity
All I can do
Is grasp for any ideas like it's air

I wish I could swim in salt water
But I know it will do more harm than good
I await when it rains
Creativity shall show up in another form
As it's droplet trickles down
Hitting me

Crumbled up Paper

It was something I couldn't forget
The feelings I felt
Frustrated
Upset
Stuck
No matter what I did
It just wasn't right

Crossing out parts
Scribbling away aggressively
Trying to remove what I didn't like
I wish I had an eraser
To remove parts of me

A bunch of rubbish
Lines of nothingness
It's not good enough
I start to take each side of the page
Crumble it up
Ready to be thrown away

"No"
The voice startling me
"Don't do that. It's valuable."
Valuable?

It's messy, it's bad

I look up
Seeing my words aren't going through
As they're too busy
Trying to flatten out the crumpled up paper

Revealing its imperfections
Seeing it to be something good
Seeing it to have worth
They see value in what I do
Value in me

Coded to be Unique

Nothing
I'll amount to nothing
It's like I'm coded to do nothing
I'm not special

We're not special
We're a part of something
A family,
A group,
A norm
We're not allowed to deviate from that

That's something we must remember
We're replaceable
Nothing important
I'm not needed

We're like code,
Made up of ones and zeros
Vast upon a screen
All blur together
So many numbers
Where am I in that?

You're in an important part

Each one of those ones and zeros make a
difference
If you remove one,
If you change one
It makes it completely different

If a single number,
can change binary code
Imagine what you can do
You have untapped power
To create
To be you
So don't get in your own way

The Forgotten Taste of Coffee

It's Sunday morning
I seem to have forgotten to collect the mail
Our mornings were our leisure time
The sound coming from the tellie,
Over playing the ringing bell

My mornings are now filled with silence
I wish I could say I'm busy
But there's much going on
I spend too much time
Thinking, debating,
Scared to ask
"How have you been?"

I hope you leave me delivered
So its okay for me to wish away my concern
For it to be temporary
Will temporary fill in the void?

My favorite song plays,
Buzz
A text, from friends, saying,
"Are you free today?"
Humming along to the tune

How childlike and sweet it is

You gave me a cup of coffee
To start each day
Energizing us
Without it
Conversations take too much from us

It's too late for coffee
As the moon is settling in
Working away,
The moon passing through its phases
I barely notice the time passing
"How long has it been?"

I reach out for a cup
Watching coffee pour
A small amount should be fine
"It's so bitter"

Time away from this drink
Time away from you
Time that made me feel empty
Your presence, linbering

Now i'm left empty
Alone by myself
You're not with me
Thoughts made me believe I was incomplete

I don't need you,
Or your bitter coffee

I'm fine without the bitterness
Perhaps I'm incomplete
But the times passes
Things will change
In my incompleteness,
I am complete

Satellite Dish

It was past 10 in the morning.
You were hitting the satellite dish,
trying to get the right channel.
I was still yawning by then.
We always missed the best parts of our show.
Switching to our next channel.
Growing impatient.

We wanted to be a simple but meaningful
picture.
A reminder of how we came to be.
I'll watch you from down here,
enjoying the view from the second floor.
You'll watch me in the back gardens,
picking apart the smells of common flowers.
Your lights were shut off, curtains closed.
But we opened up to each other.

I thought I'd miss what we had.
Simple. but meaningless.
I remember why you're gone.
A mutual decision.
I'm reminded of what you've given me.
We gave each other so much in what little we
had.

We'll look at that picture that we curated.
Put it down after a second.
We were stuck in a wheel that's meant to be
moving.
But we slowed each other down.
No longer watching each other.
Instead we'll both say we're looking at the moon

Burdensome

26

She took quiet steps,
Trying to be light
Light as a feather
Her breath however,
Was deep and heavy
Taking up too much space

Muddy Scenery

You walked towards me
 Amongst the muddy scenery
 After the rain,
 All so muted
 You with your purple umbrella
 Just you,
 Bringing the color in

You walked past me
 You didn't notice
 Perhaps I blended in the muddiness
 Maybe I wore the wrong colors

I could wear all the brightest hues
 Would I still not stand out to you?
 Amongst the gray is your blue hoodie
 But that's not your own giveaway

In the way you walk
 The way you carry yourself
 I think I could find you anywhere

Many things make up you
 From the way you part your hair
 To the temperature you like your water

I like knowing all these details about you

Knowing you is a delight
On a gloomy day you bring a bit of light
If I am dim,
You don't mind
After all, rain is just another type of weather

Taking a Chance

Here is a reminder
The words that you read
Were written by a chance
The thought comes and goes

Until they were fed up
Only coming every now and then
Waiting for it to show itself again
Wanting the idea to be used

Sometimes they don't think
No disappointment
No longing
Just simply acting

The thought comes and goes
I reached out
It took my hands
Led me here

Now you are reading my words
Some that came easily
Others I thought long and hard about
But it was a chance
It is a choice to choose

Perhaps you'll stay
You'll wonder and ponder
But you won't think of the what-ifs for so long
It comes and goes
You'll let it go

Should you follow?
Worry where you'll go
Was it worth it?
You'll see it to the end
Or you can let it go

You took a chance
You did your best
Now you are here
The end to a journey
You'll start another one
You can follow an idea and have an adventure

Binds Wearing Down

Your story and mine is a story I reread,
over and over again
Trying to remember the lines
The lines of you and I

Each syllable that comes to my mind
I read it aloud,
To see your smile
As I act out the words
Of memories we had

Your memories and mine,
fill out the lines of the pages
Of the book that we are
The book that I re-read
And re-read, and re-read
And re-read again

As you fall asleep to my voice
You and I travel to these places
Of our past
Our present
I soak in your presence
And maybe our future

As I re-read,
Re-read,
re-read
The binds of the book,
It wears down, it tears
The pages no longer brightly white as they once
were
A bit paler, older
Like the memories of you and I, together

Oh I read, I desperately read
These stories of you and I, together
You don't have the time,
Not as much anymore

You live life, you wander and ponder
The joyful life that life is
Filling up the pages of your thoughts, emotions
Leaving no room for me
You no longer have time for these stories,
and I don't have the time too

You and I are older, wiser possibly
But not young like we used to be
But the memories of what we used to be
The binds break down
Read our story once more, it will break
It's finally time to put away the book
Move on from what memories used to be

I have to let go
It is time to start a new book
A new story,
A new chapter
A new line
A new word
A new syllable

Maybe you are in this book too
Maybe you are not
Perhaps you are a recurring character
The backstory of who I used to be
You are but a memory
I will remember you in some way
Like a story from a book

The binds will finally break
The ink slowly runs off
Alas you and I are the book
The book on the bookshelf
Of what we what once used to be

Stars

I've stood in this backyard so many times before.
 It's something I can't quite call home.
 I think I'm undeserving to call it that.
 A place where I was born.
 But it's not something I can call home.
 It's comforting, nonetheless.

 The swing beside the fence used to be so scary.
 The wind pushes it slightly, and I would think it
was haunted.
 Too afraid to sit on it unless someone was with
me.
 I miss when my mind thought like a child.

 But I know better now see.
 I say that yet the shed in the corner brings me
uncertainty.
 Will it give me spiders or nightmares?
 Perhaps both.

 Let me be scared like a little kid again.
 Let my imagination run wild once more.

 I stand in the backyard.
 The wind tustles the leaves of the plum tree .

A voice, "Come inside" calling me.
But I stay put, in this place that scared me
countless times before.
But now, gives me nostalgia.
I look up and there's something I've not seen.

Stars, covering the whole sky.
There's so many stars.
So many that I can't count.
Back "home", I count the stars on one hand.
I'd still look at them with a smile.
But here? All I can do is look up, mouth wide
open.

The light pollution back "home" is so bad; the
stars you barely see.
Perhaps I took the pollution with me, carried in
my lungs.
The stars everso pretty, they breathe out the
pollution in me.
I'm like a kid once more.
The voice joins me, the stars, together we view.
My mind awestruck what my eyes see.
So all I say is, "Look at the stars" a little too
loudly.

Pen Painting Worlds

You want to be perform
Ambitious, like the person next door
Writing songs on their bedroom floor
Trying to get the syllables just right
The words fall on beat

You want to share,
Like the writer scribbling away in a notebook
So many ideas flowing through a pen
Sentences traveling,
like boats through the sea

You want to be known
People to see your movies from all over the
world
Seeing themselves in the people you play
So they can have a win
To see themselves win

You want to do so many things
But you're still here
At the very start
Afraid to take the next step

Why is that?

This is something you want
Shouldn't you give it all that you got?

I think you know deep down
You've read works
Trying to get a point across
Ideas,
Things you already knew

You still read them anyway
You're afraid
It might be different than what you expected
Different results
Go totally wrong

You knew this too
A gamble,
A chance
A risk for you to be you

Its okay to be scared
Be scared and move,
Pick up a pen
Go start
You'll be in a different world
One you painted yourself